THE
BRITISH
MUSEUM Pocket Timeline of

Ancient Mesopotamia

Katharine Wiltshire

THE BRITISH MUSEUM PRESS

© 2005 The Trustees of the British Museum

Katharine Wiltshire has asserted the right to be identified as the author of this work.

First published in Great Britain in 2005 by
British Museum Press
A division of the British Museum Company Ltd
38 Russell Square, London WC1B 3QQ

ISBN-10: 0-7141-3113-X
ISBN-13: 978-0-7141-3113-9

A catalogue record for this title is available from the British Library.

Designed and typeset by Peter Bailey for Proof Books
Printed in China

Illustration acknowledgements

All photographs are © the Trustees of the British Museum, taken by the British Museum Photography and Imaging Dept, unless otherwise stated.

Map on p. 31 by ML Design

Richard Ashworth/Robert Harding: p. 11 top;
p. 23 bottom.
www.bridgeman.co.uk: p. 18 top.
Astrid and Hanns-Frieder Michler/Science Photo Library:
p. 5 top.
B. Norman/Ancient Art & Architecture Collection: p. 17.
Jane Sweeney/Lonely Planet Images: p. 30 bottom.
Victoria Theakston/Robert Harding World Imagery:
p. 4 bottom.

CONTENTS

Early Mesopotamia   4

     First cities   7

Sumer   8

     Farming   10

     Uruk   11

     Writing   12

     Cities and empires   14

Akkadian empire   15

Third Dynasty of Ur   16

     Buildings   18

     Arts and crafts   19

Babylonian period   20

     Religion   22

     Ziggurats   23

Assyrian empire   24

     Learning   26

Neo-Babylonian empire   27

Later History   29

Map of Mesopotamia   31

Further Reading   32

Timeline of Ancient Mesopotamia   After page 32

EARLY MESOPOTAMIA

This object is known as an eye idol because of the large eyes carved on it. It comes from the site of an important prehistoric city known today as Tell Brak.

MESOPOTAMIA IS THE LAND between the River Euphrates and the River Tigris. At the end of the last Ice Age, about 12,000 years ago, the climate in Mesopotamia began to warm up and the rainfall increased. In the north there was grassland, while to the south there was a desert landscape. The region was home to many species of wild animals and plants. Both the River Euphrates and the River Tigris frequently flooded the surrounding land. (Today the floods are controlled by dams.) Each time the floodwater went down, it left behind a layer of silt, creating a fertile area of soil near the rivers. At this early time both rivers flowed directly into the sea (later known as the Persian Gulf).

The first people to live in Mesopotamia led a nomadic life. They moved from one temporary campsite to another and

This photograph shows the landscape of southern Mesopotamia, which has changed little since ancient times.

4

lived by hunting animals and gathering wild plants. Then, around 6000 BC, people began to keep animals and grow their own food crops on the fertile river soil in northern Mesopotamia. These first farmers settled in one place and lived in small villages. They grew wild cereal plants and kept sheep and goats. Around 5500 BC, irrigation was developed. This meant river water was carried in canals and ditches to water the soil in regions where there was not much rain. Farmers were now able to settle in central and southern Mesopotamia where there was little rainfall. They built earth banks and dug ditches to channel water from the rivers to the fields. Many farming villages grew up near the River Euphrates on the fertile soil left by the floods.

Early farmers cultivated wild cereals such as wheat and barley.

This stone vessel, carved in about 3100 BC, shows domesticated bulls.

This painted pottery bowl dates to about 5500 BC. Before the invention of the potter's wheel, pottery such as this was made by hand.

These early villages existed in what is known today as the prehistoric period, before the invention of writing. Because of this we do not know what these people called themselves. Nowadays, archaeologists divide this period of Mesopotamian prehistory into groups (called cultures) based on pottery styles and named after the sites where they were first identified. An example of one of these cultures is the Ubaid. This culture flourished from about 5900 BC to 4300 BC. The Ubaid people built their villages in the south of Mesopotamia. They irrigated their crops with water from the River Euphrates, kept sheep, goats and pigs and lived in houses made from mud bricks. Their potters made white pots, with bold patterns, and clay figurines. The pottery of the later Ubaid culture spread to northern Mesopotamia.

Cows were one of the first wild animals to be domesticated by early farmers. This frieze came from a temple at Al-Ubaid near Ur. It dates from c. 2500 BC.

FIRST CITIES

The early Mesopotamian farming villages were so productive that, as some of the villages grew into towns, many people were able to live in the town without having to farm for themselves. This meant that some people were able to work full time as scribes, metalworkers, potters, weavers or bakers. Some towns were able to develop into large cities, surrounded by farmland which provided the food for the people living in these cities. Cities could also trade some of their produce for goods which they could not grow or make themselves.

Across Mesopotamia, different groups of people emerged, based around particular cities. The Sumerians were to be found in southern Mesopotamia, the Akkadians, and then the Babylonians, in central Mesopotamia and the Assyrians in northern Mesopotamia. Sometimes, the whole of Mesopotamia was ruled by one of these groups of people. Sometimes, it was ruled by people who came from outside Mesopotamia.

This stone statue is of Kurlil, a royal official from the Sumerian city of Uruk. He was responsible for the building work at the temple of the goddess Ninhursag at al-Ubaid in about 2500 BC.

This statuette of a goat comes from a tomb in the city of Ur. It shows the skilled work being undertaken by craftspeople living in the cities of Mesopotamia about 2600 BC.

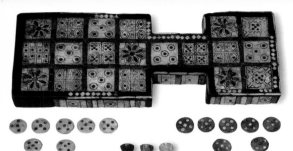

SUMER

THE SOUTHERN REGION of Mesopotamia was known as Sumer. From about 3000 BC, settlements in Sumer began to grow into large cities. Sumer's first city was Uruk, which was built alongside the River Euphrates. Other early cities in Sumer were Eridu, Ur, Larsa, Lagash, Isin, Adad, Nippur and Kish.

The Royal Game of Ur was found in the Royal Cemetery. It is a board game in which two players race to get their counters around the squares on the board.

Each city was governed by its own ruler and surrounded by farmland which provided food for the people who lived in the city. Sometimes, one of these cities would become particularly powerful and would rule the other cities around it. Sometimes, such a city was powerful enough to rule all Mesopotamia. One such city was Ur, which began as a village in about 4500 BC. By 2500 BC it had grown into a large city of about 20,000 people. Ur was built in southern Mesopotamia near the River Euphrates. The city was packed with houses, shops and markets with a huge temple complex at the centre. The city

This stone carving shows Enannatum, ruler of the city of Lagash, one of the most important city-states in Sumer.

was served by an irrigation system which brought water from the river to water the city's farmland, and it had two harbours where trading boats could unload. Ships could sail down the river to the Persian Gulf. The city's merchants traded as far away as the Indian subcontinent.

The Sumerian cities were home to merchants, scribes, craftspeople, priests and priestesses. Farmers and fishermen lived on the surrounding land. The south of Mesopotamia was much drier than the north and Sumerian farmers used irrigation to carry water from the rivers to their crops and animals. The Sumerians invented a system of writing to record information about farming and trading. Gradually writing came to be used to record other things, and by 2700 BC, legends and myths were being written down. The early writing surfaces were stone and small clay tablets. Many aspects of Sumerian culture were absorbed into the culture of the peoples who succeeded them as rulers of Sumer and Mesopotamia.

This shell plaque from Ur was probably used to decorate the sound-box of a lyre.

The Standard of Ur is beautifully decorated with inlaid pictures. This side shows a banquet scene.

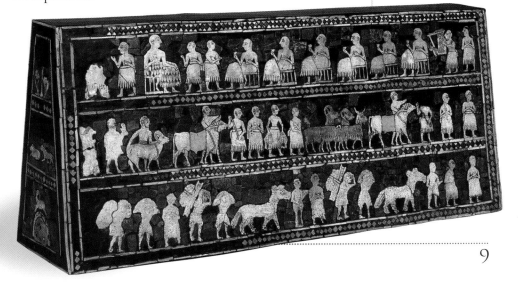

Sheep were among the first animals domesticated by early farmers. This sheep's head was made about 3100 BC.

FARMING

Sumerian farmers grew barley, wheat and emmer (a type of wheat). Farming was carefully controlled. A clay tablet has been found at Ur which describes each stage of arable farming, from the preparation of a field to the harvesting of the crop. Vegetables were grown in gardens, shielded from the heat and wind by rows of trees.

New tools were invented to help farmers with their crops, such as sickles for harvesting the wheat and barley, and ploughs to till the fields. People discovered how to build ovens to bake bread made from ground grain. They learned how to extract linen thread from the flax plant and use this flax to weave cloth for clothes, bedding and sails. Wool was also spun and then woven. Mesopotamia had little stone or wood so people learned to use river clay to make things. They used clay to make bricks for building, vessels for storing and serving food, and clay tablets for writing on.

This clay tablet records barley rations distributed at the temple of Bau, near the city of Lagash, about 2350 BC.

URUK

Uruk was the earliest Sumerian city and probably the first city in all Mesopotamia. As the city grew it spread out across the plain near the River Euphrates. The city had a large population. It was a major religious centre and contained two temples, one dedicated to the god An and the other to the goddess Inanna.

The people of Uruk used pictograms (simple picture symbols which represented objects) to record the animals and crops that were being produced on the surrounding farmland. The city was able to grow so large because of the amount of good farmland it controlled, because it was close to trade routes in the region and because it occupied a good position on the banks of the River Euphrates. From about 3000 BC onwards, the changes which had occurred in Uruk were happening at other settlements across southern Mesopotamia.

This photograph shows the site of the ancient city of Uruk.

This early cylinder seal probably comes from the city of Uruk. It is made from white limestone. The impression shows a priest-king and four animals.

This clay tablet was used by an apprentice scribe learning to write cuneiform in about 1800 BC.

WRITING

Writing began in the Sumerian cities, possibly the city of Uruk, around 3100 BC. This writing was used to record the collection and distribution of food supplies in the cities and the business activities of merchants. The first Sumerian writing used pictograms. Pictograms are simple pictures which represent objects. Gradually, these pictograms were simplified into a form of writing which used wedge-shapes. This writing is known as cuneiform. Cuneiform signs were quicker to write than pictograms and, as well as representing objects, they could express ideas. Individual cuneiform signs represented syllables which could be combined to make a word, or used by themselves to represent a complete word. Eventually, there were more than 600 cuneiform signs. The first cuneiform represented the Sumerian language. Later, the Akkadians, Assyrians and Babylonians and many others wrote down their languages using cuneiform.

Cylinder seals were invented in Mesopotamia at about the same time as writing. They were used as a way to mark property. This seal was in the tomb of a woman called Pu-abi, who lived c. 2600 BC.

Most of the writing from Mesopotamia is on small clay tablets. Damp clay was formed into a flat tablet, which could be held in one hand. The writer pressed a stylus made from reed, wood, metal or ivory into the clay to make the cuneiform signs, then left the tablet in the sun to harden. Early numbers were recorded by making circular or semi-circular marks in the surface of a clay tablet with the other end of the stylus. Later cuneiform signs were used for a counting system based on 60. From about 1300 BC, ivory and wooden tablets covered with a layer of wax were also used for writing. These could be reused, since the wax could be smoothed over ready for the next piece of writing. Cuneiform signs were also carved onto stone and metal. Cuneiform was used in Mesopotamia for over 3000 years. The last known use of cuneiform is a second-century AD Babylonian astronomy text.

This cuneiform tablet is a letter sent by the Babylonian king Burnaburriash to the Egyptian pharaoh Amenhotep IV (reigned c. 1352 - 1336 BC).

This stela shows the Assyrian king Ashurbanipal. The writing records the work that the king had carried out on a temple about 660 BC.

CITIES AND EMPIRES

Sumer's first cities and the land surrounding them were independent city-states each with its own ruler. However, as the cities grew wealthy from trade, they started to compete with each other for control over the whole of Sumer. Later, different peoples created empires in Mesopotamia which controlled large areas of land together with the cities. Within these empires, particular cities would be chosen as the capital city. One such city was the city of Babylon, built on the banks of the River Euphrates. The river ran through the middle of the city and a bridge linked the two halves. The city was home to the Babylonian kings as well as being the commercial, political and religious centre for the Babylonian empire. The first capital city of the Assyrian people was at Ashur on the River Tigris. Later, their capital moved to Kalhu (now known as Nimrud), then to Dur-Sharrakin (Khorsabad) and then to Nineveh.

The writing on this stela includes a description of the building of the city of Kalhu (Nimrud). It was set up by king Ashurnasirpal II (reigned 883-859 BC).

This circular brick is inscribed with cuneiform writing which tells us that it came from a temple built in the Sumerian city of Lagash about 2100 BC.

AKKADIAN EMPIRE

C. 2334 TO C. 2193 BC

IN ABOUT 2400 BC, the Akkadians, a Semitic people who had lived alongside the Sumerians, gained control of Mesopotamia and founded a capital city at Agade in central Mesopotamia. Under their leader Sargon I (reigned *c.* 2334 - 2279 BC) they captured many Sumerian cities and established an Akkadian empire. At its greatest extent, under Sargon's grandson Naram-Sin (reigned *c.* 2254 - 2218 BC), the Akkadian empire stretched from the Mediterranean Sea to the Persian Gulf.

This bronze tankard dates from about 200 years after the Akkadian empire, but the inscription is written in Akkadian cuneiform.

The Akkadians adopted the Sumerian system of writing, though Akkadian became the official language for written documents, replacing the Sumerians' own language. The Akkadians took over some of the Sumerians' ideas about government and some of their gods and goddesses. Mesopotamia was ruled by the Akkadians until about 2193 BC, when the Akkadians lost control of all their lands except their capital city of Agade.

This Akkadian cylinder seal and impression probably show a scene from a myth about the Zu bird and the god Ea. The seal dates from around 2300 BC.

THIRD DYNASTY OF UR

WITH THE END of the Akkadian empire, the Sumerian cities in southern Mesopotamia went back to being independent and powerful new kings emerged to rule the cities. Some of these kings were able to gain control of other Sumerian cities. One such king was Gudea, king of the Sumerian city of Lagash. He revived old trade routes and restored old temples. Then, around 2110 BC, king Ur-Nammu of Ur (reigned *c.* 2112 - 2095 BC) reunited all the Sumerian cities. He was proclaimed 'King of Sumer and Akkad'. He restored temples and began to build tall stepped towers, known as ziggurats, as part of the temple complexes. This period of Mesopotamian history is known as the Third Dynasty of Ur after the main city at this time – Ur. It is also sometimes known as the Neo-Sumerian period.

This bronze figure represents Ur-Nammu, the ruler of Ur from about 2112 to 2095 BC. Ur-Nammu is shown lifting up a basket of earth for making bricks.

A cylinder seal and modern impression naming king Shulgi (reigned *c.* 2094-2047 BC). The central figure is probably a royal official called Kilula.

Ur-Nammu's son Shulgi (reigned *c.* 2094 - 2047 BC) created an empire which controlled the whole of Mesopotamia by means of a huge administration. However, such a large empire was difficult to control and gradually the conquered cities broke free and returned to self-rule. In 2004 BC, the city of Ur was invaded by the Elamites from the east and by the Amorites from the west. The fate of Ibbi-Sin, the last Sumerian king, is unknown.

As the power of the Third Dynasty of Ur collapsed, the region entered a period of unrest. Groups of people moved across Mesopotamia in search of places to live. The Amorites settled in Mesopotamia and took control of the Sumerian cities. Under the Amorites each major city was ruled by its own king and the region was broken up into a number of small kingdoms. The cities of Isin and Larsa were the dominant powers.

This photograph shows the site of the city of Ur.

Buildings

As the Mesopotamian villages grew into towns, and then cities, so the number and types of buildings increased. Most Mesopotamian buildings were built using timber and mud bricks. These bricks were made from river mud, which was shaped into a brick and then dried in the sun. The mud-brick walls were plastered and often whitewashed.

A modern, half-size reconstruction of the Ishtar Gate from Babylon. The original gate was built about 680 BC.

Some houses in the cities were two stories high and built facing into a central courtyard. A city also contained the royal palace, temples, workshops, shops and schools. High walls were built around the cities to protect them from floods and attack. The most important temples were decorated with sculptures, and the walls of some palaces were painted. In the first millennium, some Assyrian kings decorated their palaces with carved stone wall reliefs.

This is one of a pair of guardian figures which flanked one of the entrances to a small temple dedicated to the goddess Ishtar near a royal palace at Kalhu (Nimrud) about 665 BC.

ARTS AND CRAFTS

Mesopotamian cities were home to specialist craftworkers. These workers used a wide range of materials to create different craft and art objects. Mesopotamian pottery included bowls, plates, saucers and jars. At first pottery was shaped by hand. Then, from about 3400 BC, the potter's wheel was introduced, enabling potters to make pots with thinner sides and in more elaborate shapes. Many pots were left undecorated. Others were decorated with a thin wash of coloured liquid clay, burnished (polished so that they had a shiny surface) or painted with patterns. The process of making glass was perfected in Mesopotamia about 1600 BC and by the 700s BC a wide range of glass vessels was being produced. A variety of stones were used to make statues, cylinder seals and carved wall reliefs. There was no stone in the south and little in the north, and there were no metal mines in Mesopotamia, so both materials had to be imported. Copper, bronze, silver and gold were used to make weapons, farming equipment, cups, vases, dishes, bowls and jewellery. Metal was also used to decorate objects made from other materials such as wooden musical instruments and stone statues.

This Sumerian lyre is richly decorated with gold, lapis lazuli, shell and red limestone. It dates from around 2600 BC.

This fluted glass bottle dates to around 1300 BC. Glass was one of the earliest artificial materials made by humans.

19

OLD BABYLONIAN PERIOD

This fragment of a stone stela shows king Hammurabi. It dates from the end of his reign.

C. 2004 TO C. 1595 BC

AROUND 2004 BC, the Amorites, a Semitic people from the west of Mesopotamia, invaded Sumer and established several city-states. In 1894 BC, Babylon became the capital city of an Amorite leader called Sumu-abum. He was the first of a long line of kings who ruled the city. Then, in about 1792 BC, Hammurabi became king of Babylon. He reigned until about 1750 BC. He conquered cities in north and south Mesopotamia and made Babylon the capital city of a Babylonian empire. One of his most important acts was to draw up a set of laws, some of which were based on older Sumerian laws. This has become known as Hammurabi's law-code and it

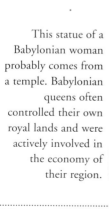

This statue of a Babylonian woman probably comes from a temple. Babylonian queens often controlled their own royal lands and were actively involved in the economy of their region.

20

demonstrated his commitment to justice across the Babylonian empire. One copy of the code, written in cuneiform on a large stone stela, was carried off by the Elamites during the 13th century BC to the city of Susa. It is now in the Louvre Museum in Paris.

This cylinder seal belonged to Sin-ishmeanni, who worked for a ruler in northern Babylonia about 1850 BC. The impression shows the owner standing between a seated king and a standing goddess.

After Hammurabi, the power of the Babylonian empire began to decline. Cities which were part of the empire rebelled and people from outside the empire invaded it. A Hittite raid from Anatolia in about 1595 BC brought about the downfall of the First Dynasty of Babylon, and a Kassite king, Agum-Kakrime, seized the throne of Babylon for himself. The Kassites went on to rule Babylon for a further 450 years. They maintained the Babylonian way of life, respected the Mesopotamian gods, and rebuilt their temples. They built a large new city at Dur Kurigalzu in central Mesopotamia, though they kept Babylon as the capital city for the region.

This Babylonian terracotta mould shows a horse and rider. Moulds like this were made in large numbers.

Religion

The people of Mesopotamia believed that the universe was controlled by gods and goddesses who had to be obeyed and worshipped with prayers and offerings. There were many myths and legends about these gods and goddesses. Temples were the centres of religious activity where priests and priestesses served a particular god or goddess. People believed that the god or goddess lived in the temple. All temples contained a statue of their god or goddess, together with an offering table. Special feasts and festivals were held in honour of the gods and goddesses. The ancient Mesopotamians believed in a life after death. At some periods, important people were buried with some of the possessions and food they believed they would need in the afterlife.

This carved stone relief, dating from around 865 BC, stood at an entrance to the throne room in a royal place at Kalhu (Nimrud). It probably shows a protective spirit known as an *apkallu*.

This small limestone statue shows a woman worshipping one of the Sumerian gods. These statues were placed in temple to pray on the donor's behalf. This statue dates from around 2500 BC.

ZIGGURATS

In the courtyards of some ancient Mesopotamian temples there were tall, stepped structures known as ziggurats. Ziggurats were built from layers of mud bricks, protected by baked bricks on the exterior, and held together with reed matting at regular intervals to provide drainage. They rose in square or rectangular platforms to a sacred shrine at the top. Each platform was smaller than the one below and long ramps or flights of stairs were used to climb up from one platform to the next. The first ziggurats were built by king Ur-Nammu (reigned *c.* 2112 - 2095 BC) in the Sumerian cities of Ur, Eridu, Nippur and Uruk. A ziggurat dedicated to the Mesopotamian god Marduk may have been built at Babylon about 1750 BC. By the time of king Nebuchadnezzar II (reigned 605 - 562 BC) it had seven platforms of bricks with a temple for Marduk on the summit. The ziggurat at Dur Sharrukin, built by the Assyrians about 710 BC, possibly had a spiral ramp leading to the top, with each platform of bricks painted a different colour.

This cylinder seal impression shows some of the principal gods and goddesses of Mesopotamia in about 2300 BC, including Ishtar, Shamash, Ea and Usimu.

The ziggurat at Ur was dedicated to the moon god Nanna in about 2100 BC. It originally had three platforms. This is a modern restoration of the first stage.

ASSYRIAN EMPIRE

C. 870 TO C. 612 BC In the north of
Mesopotamia the Assyrian people had established
a kingdom, with its main city at Ashur in the
valley of the River Tigris. In 1363 BC Ashuruballit I became king of Assyria. He conquered
part of Mitanni, which lay to the west of Assyria,
and made contact with Egypt. During the 9th
century BC, the Assyrian kings began to expand
their kingdom and gradually took control of all of
Mesopotamia. Under king Ashurnasirpal II, Assyria's empire
stretched to the west of Mesopotamia as far as the
Mediterranean Sea. Ashurnasirpal moved the capital to Kalhu
(now known as Nimrud). He built a wall around the city
and built a royal palace and temple complex on top of an
ancient mound. There the kings of Assyria lived for almost
200 years. A later Assyrian king, Sargon, made Dur
Sharrukin (Khorsabad) his capital, but his son king
Sennacherib (reigned 704-681 BC) made Nineveh the new
capital. Nineveh was twice as big
as Nimrud. Sennacherib
had canals built to carry
water into the city and
its farmland, and
constructed a grand
royal palace. Around the
palace he established a
park full of exotic
plants and animals.

This glazed tile comes
from a royal palace at
Kalhu (Nimrud). It
shows the Assyrian
king Ashurnasirpal II
(reigned 883 - 859 BC)
with his attendants.

This bronze weight
was made in the
shape of a lion in
about 800 BC.

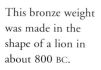

By 650 BC, under the rule of king Ashurbanipal, the Assyrian empire was at its greatest extent, stretching from Mesopotamia across to the Mediterranean Sea and south to Egypt. However, when Ashurbanipal died in 631 BC the Assyrian empire fell apart. People invaded from outside the empire and cities and regions within the empire rebelled. In 612 BC, the Babylonians and Medes revolted against Assyrian rule, attacking and destroying all the major Assyrian cities including Nineveh. They divided the Assyrian empire between them and the Assyrians were never strong enough to rule Mesopotamia again.

This highly decorated bronze bowl was found in the palace of Ashurnasirpal II (reigned 883-859 BC) at Kalhu (Nimrud). The bowl originally came from Syria.

Most Assyrian palace reliefs were carved between 870 BC and 620 BC. This relief, which dates from around 645 BC, shows two Mesopotamian lions. This stone relief originally decorated the walls of a royal palace at Nineveh.

A Babylonian map of the world, made about 600 BC. The city of Babylon is marked in the centre with all the known lands around it. The circle represents the sea. The vertical lines are probably the River Euphrates.

This stone tablet records building work at a temple during the reign of king Nabu-apla-iddina. It was discovered 250 years later by king Nabopolassar (reigned 625 - 605 BC).

LEARNING

Mesopotamian cities were centres of knowledge and learning. The first schools were places where scribes were taught to become administrators. Later these schools started to teach botany, zoology, geography, mathematics and astronomy. The Sumerians developed a number system based on 60. The Assyrians occasionally used a system based on 10. To help with mathematical calculations, people used multiplication tables written on clay tablets. Surveying with measuring instruments was used to help build irrigation systems.

Babylonian astronomers studied the night sky and recorded the movement of the moon and planets. The Assyrian king Ashurbanipal (reigned 668 - 631 BC) collected a library of about 25,000 clay tablets at his palace at Nineveh.

The tablets included letters, legends, dictionaries, histories, astronomical observations, and medical texts. The Babylonian king Nebuchadnezzar II (reigned 605 - 562 BC) started a 'museum' in Babylon, which contained objects and statues from distant corners of his empire, some dating from earlier periods.

NEO-BABYLONIAN EMPIRE

As the power of the Assyrians declined the Chaldean people, from southern Mesopotamia, began to create their own empire. This empire was later known as the Late Babylonian or Neo-Babylonian empire. In 625 BC the Chaldean king Nabopolassar captured the city of Babylon from the Assyrians and made it part of his empire. His son, Nebuchadnezzar II (reigned 605 - 562 BC), rebuilt and enlarged Babylon and made it the capital city of the empire. He rebuilt a great seven-storey ziggurat in Babylon. At this time Babylon covered about 405 hectares (1000 acres) and was surrounded by a massive 17-kilometre (10.6 mile) wall. The royal palace was so grand that Nebuchadnezzar called it 'the marvel of all people, the centre of the land, the shining residence, the dwelling of majesty'. He also built the Hanging Gardens of Babylon. This was a terraced garden full of trees and flowering plants, built to remind his wife, Queen Amyitis, of the green hills of her homeland in Media. It was one of the Seven Wonders of the Ancient World.

It has been estimated that 15 million bricks were used to rebuild the official buildings in Babylon during the reign of Nebuchadnezzar II. They were usually square and marked with a cuneiform stamp.

This clay cylinder describes the three palaces which Nebuchadnezzar had built in Babylon. It was buried beneath the walls of the palace and was intended to be read by future kings when the palace had to be repaired.

This cuneiform tablet is part of the chronicle recording events during the reign of king Nabonidus. It says that the king spent ten years campaigning, leaving his son Bel-shar-usur in charge.

After Nebuchadnezzar's reign the Neo-Babylonian empire gradually went into decline and over the next twenty years it began to break up. Eventually, the area controlled by the city of Babylon was reduced to the land immediately around the city itself. Meanwhile the Persians, who came from the regions to the east of Mesopotamia, were extending their control. In 539 BC the Persian king Cyrus captured Babylon and made it and the rest of Mesopotamia part of the Achaemenid Persian empire. The Neo-Babylonian empire had fallen.

This stone stela shows the last king of the Neo-Babylonian empire, king Nabonidus (reigned 555 - 539 BC).

LATER HISTORY

MESOPOTAMIA BECAME part of the Persian empire in 539 BC. Two hundred years later, the Persian empire was conquered by the Macedonian ruler Alexander the Great. He made Mesopotamia part of his empire. After Alexander's death in Babylon in 323 BC, his empire was divided up and Mesopotamia was ruled by the Seleucid dynasty founded by Seleukos, one of Alexander's generals. Then, in 141 BC, the Parthian king Mithradates I took control of Mesopotamia. The Parthians, who came from eastern Iran, briefly lost control of Mesopotamia when it was invaded by the Romans in AD 115 but it was returned to the Parthians by the Roman emperor Hadrian in AD 117.

This bronze buckle shows a Parthian horse rider. It dates from around the 2nd century AD.

Bronze head of the Roman emperor Hadrian. Mesopotamia was briefly a part of the Roman empire before Hadrian returned it to the Parthians.

The Parthian empire was overthrown by the Sasanian king Ardashir in AD 224 - 26. Mesopotamia was then ruled by Sasanian kings, also from Iran, until AD 637, when Muslim Arabs invaded and Mesopotamia became part of their Islamic empire. From AD 1534 until 1918 Mesopotamia was part of the Ottoman empire, ruled by the Ottoman dynasty who ruled from Istanbul in modern Turkey. Nowadays, most of Mesopotamia is the country of Iraq with its capital city at Baghdad, in central Mesopotamia.

This coin shows the Sasanian king Ardashir I (reigned AD 224 - 41). His crown copies the style of those of the previous Parthian kings who ruled over Mesopotamia.

Baghdad is the capital city of modern Iraq. The city was founded in AD 762 on the banks of the River Tigris.

FURTHER READING

MESOPOTAMIA AND THE
ANCIENT NEAR EAST
John Malam
Evans, 1999

MESOPOTAMIA
Jen Green and Lorna Oakes
Southwater, 2003

STEP INTO ANCIENT MESOPOTAMIA
Lorna Oakes
Lorenz Books, 2001

FIRST CIVILIZATIONS
Erica Hunter and Mike Corbishley
Facts on File, 2003

Some useful websites:

The British Museum
The main British Museum website can be found at
www.thebritishmuseum.ac.uk

The British Museum's interactive learning site about ancient Mesopotamia
can be found at **www.mesopotamia.co.uk**

COMPASS
COMPASS allows you to browse the British Museum's collection on line,
with thousands of images and background information about objects and
the people who made and used them. COMPASS also features a wide range
of tours about the Museum's exhibitions and other themes.
www.thebritishmuseum.ac.uk/compass

CHILDREN'S COMPASS
There are hundreds of objects from around the world on Children's
COMPASS. Find out about different cultures from across time and compare
key themes based around everyday life, belief, technology and rulers.
www.thebritishmuseum.ac.uk/childrenscompass

MAP

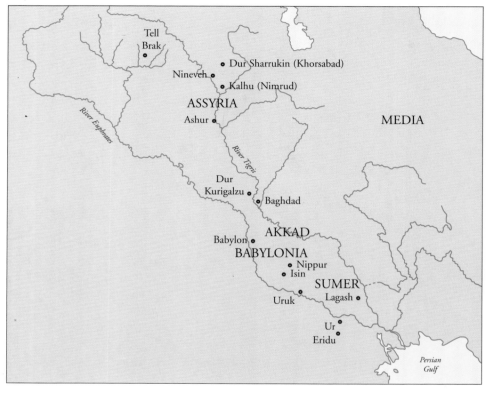

A map of ancient Mesopotamia, showing the important sites mentioned in this book.

THE BRITISH MUSEUM

Pocket Timeline of Ancient Mesopotamia

T HIS TIMELINE tells you about the key periods, people and events of ancient Mesopotamia. Each column covers 200 years of history, except for the first column, which deals with Mesopotamian history before 2300 BC, and the last two columns, which cover some of the years after 300 BC.

Most of the dates on the timeline are followed by the letters BC. These letters stand for 'Before Christ'. This indicates that the year comes before the date traditionally given for the birth of Jesus Christ – the year AD 1. Years which occur after the birth of Christ have the letters AD in front of them. These letters stand for the Latin phrase *Anno Domini*, meaning 'In the year of our Lord'.

Sometimes, it is not known exactly when an event happened. In this case, 'c.' appears before the year. This stands for the Latin word *circa*, which means 'about'.

SUMER 3100 BC – 2300 BC

■ c. 6500 – 4300 BC
Groups of people belonging to the Ubaid, Hassuna, Samara and Halaf cultures live in Mesopotamia.

■ c. 6000 BC
First farming and first hand-made pottery in the ancient Near East.

■ c. 4300 – 2900 BC
People belonging to the Uruk culture live in southern Mesopotamia.

■ c. 3500 BC
First wheel-made pottery.

■ c. 3200 BC
First picture writing is used in Mesopotamia.

■ c. 3100 BC
First cuneiform writing.

A clay tablet with pictographs recording food supplies.

■ From c. 3000 BC
First cities in Sumer.

■ c. 2600 BC
Rulers of the First and Second Dynasties of Ur are buried in the city's Royal Cemetery.

The Royal Standard of Ur, from a tomb in the Royal Cemetery.

This Akkadian cylinder seal and its modern impression show some of the principal Mesopotamian gods and goddesses.

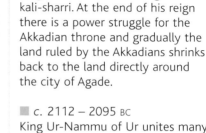

■ *c.* 2217 – 2193 BC
Reign of the Akkadian king Shar-kali-sharri. At the end of his reign there is a power struggle for the Akkadian throne and gradually the land ruled by the Akkadians shrinks back to the land directly around the city of Agade.

■ *c.* 2334 – 2279 BC
Reign of Akkadian king Sargon, ruler of the city of Agade in central Mesopotamia. During his reign the Akkadians take control of the cities in the region, leading to the creation of an Akkadian empire.

■ *c.* 2112 – 2095 BC
King Ur-Nammu of Ur unites many of the cities of southern Mesopotamia under his rule and founds the Third Dynasty of Ur. He rebuilds old cities and constructs ziggurats in honour of gods and goddesses.

■ *c.* 2254 – 2218 BC
Reign of the Akkadian king Naram-Sin. During his reign the Akkadian empire reaches its greatest extent.

The restored first stage of the ziggurat at Ur.

A cuneiform tablet recording barley rations at the temple dedicated to the goddess of Bau in Girsu, near the city of Lagash.

■ *c.* 2112 – 2095 BC
The ziggurat at Ur is built on the site of an older and smaller ziggurat. It has three platforms and a system of broad stairways.

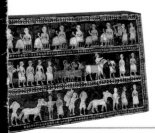

■ *c.* 2100 BC
A ziggurat is built in Uruk as part of an existing temple complex.

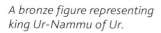

A bronze figure representing king Ur-Nammu of Ur.

■ *c.* 2094 – 2047 BC
Reign of king Shulgi of the Third Dynasty of Ur. He undertakes major administrative reforms and tens of thousands of cuneiform tablets survive from his reign. During his reign a great royal mausoleum (tomb) is constructed just outside the city walls.

The middle figure on this cylinder seal impression is perhaps king Shulgi.

■ *c.* 2004 BC
The Third Dynasty of Ur ends. Supply routes across the empire are disrupted by the Amorite people. Then the Elamites, who come from east of Mesopotamia, destroy the city of Ur, and the king is taken into exile. The Amorite people settle in Sumer and take control of the Sumerian cities. Each major city is once again ruled by its own individual king.

A cuneiform letter (right) and its sealed clay envelope (left) from Kanesh.

■ *c.* 1940 – 1740 BC
The city of Ashur on the west bank of the River Tigris in northern Mesopotamia grows in size and power. The city is governed by local rulers and the Assyrian people grow wealthy from trade.

■ *c.* 1920 BC
Assyrian merchants from the city of Ashur establish a trading colony at the foot of the city mound of Kanesh in central Anatolia (now Kültepe in modern Turkey). Tin and textiles are carried from Ashur to the trading colony to be exchanged for Anatolian gold and silver. Large archives of cuneiform tablets have been found at Kanesh.

A stone seal from Anatolia dating from the time of trade between Assyria and Anatolia.

A statue of a Babylonian woman.

c. 1894 BC
Babylon in central Mesopotamia becomes the capital of a small Amorite city-state under the rule of king Sumu-abum.

c. 1813 – 1781 BC
The Amorite leader Shamshi-Adad I conquers much of northern Mesopotamia. He puts his son Iasmah-Addu on the throne of the city of Mari on the River Euphrates. Archives of cuneiform letters have been found in Mari which reveal much about this period of Mesopotamian history.

A clay tablet used for practising cuneiform.

c. 1792 – 1750 BC
Reign of the Babylonian king Hammurabi, who conquers much of Mesopotamia and creates a Babylonian empire. The people in the empire have many different traditions and laws so Hammurabi issues a single Law Code to help him rule them all. Between 1764 and 1760 Hammurabi extends the power of the First Dynasty of Babylon throughout Mesopotamia.

Stela fragment showing king Hammurabi.

c. 1781 – 1740 BC
Reign of Ishme-Dagan, king of northern Mesopotamia. During his reign he loses control of much of the land ruled by his father Shamshi-Adad I to king Hammurabi of Babylon and his kingdom is reduced to the land around the cities of Ashur and Nineveh.

c. 1749 – 1712 BC
Reign of the Babylonian king Samsu-iluna. During his reign the Kassite people, who later rule Babylon and create their own Kassite empire, are first mentioned in Babylonian records.

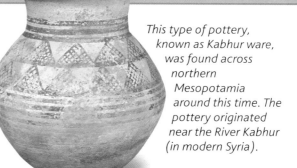

c. 1680 BC
The Hurrian people from eastern Anatolia (modern Turkey) establish themselves in northern Mesopotamia and Syria. Eventually these people create a huge empire, known as the Mitannian empire, which includes all of northern Mesopotamia.

This type of pottery, known as Kabhur ware, was found across northern Mesopotamia around this time. The pottery originated near the River Kabhur (in modern Syria).

c. 1600 BC
Mesopotamians begin to make glass.

c. 1595 BC
The first Babylonian empire ends after Babylon is attacked by the Hittites from Anatolia, under their king Mursili I.

1595 – 1155 BC
Babylonia is ruled by Kassite rulers. It is thought that the Kassites came from the Zagros Mountains to the north-east of Babylonia. The Kassites remain as rulers of Babylonia for about 400 years. The Kassites rebuild many Babylonian cities and build a new city called Dur Kurigalzu (near modern Baghdad) where they construct a huge ziggurat.

A terracotta mould of a horse and rider from Old Babylonian times, when horses became more common in Mesopotamia.

This clay tablet includes a story explaining how the Babylonians believed the universe was organized by their gods.

■ *c.* 1500 BC
Northern Mesopotamia, including the cities of Ashur and Nineveh, is part of the Mittani empire. At its greatest extent the Mittani empire stretches from northern Mesopotamia across to the Mediterranean Sea. Eventually, the empire is divided between the Hittites in the west and the Assyrians in the east.

■ *c.* 1415 BC
Historical records begin again in Babylon after a 200 year period when the city had declined in power. At this time the city is ruled by Kassite kings. The Kassite kings unite the cities of central and southern Mesopotamia and create a Kassite empire which lasts until 1154 BC. The Kassites set up close trading links with Egypt.

■ *c.* 1400 BC
The Assyrians become more independent of the Mittani empire as the region around the city of Ashur grows more powerful.

A Mitannian pottery jar.

■ *c.* 1363 BC
King Ashuruballit I defeats the Mitannians and rules an independent Assyrian kingdom from Ashur.

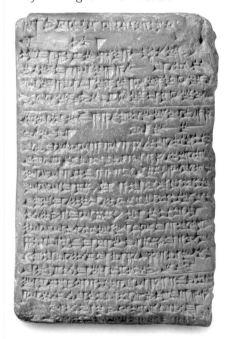

An Amarna letter.

■ *c.* 1350 BC
Cuneiform tablets found in Egypt, and known nowadays as the Amarna letters, are exchanged between the Kassite rulers of Babylon, the king of Assyria and the pharaohs of Egypt.

An Assyrian cylinder seal and its impression, showing a lion and a winged horse.

■ c. 1243 – 1207 BC
The Assyrian king Tukulti-Ninurta I extends the Assyrian empire from the Tigris Valley across to the River Euphrates. At one point he even controls land down to the Persian Gulf, though the power of the Assyrian empire declines after his death.

This mask was found in the city of Ur. It possibly comes from a religious statue. Similar masks have also been found in northern Mesopotamia.

A Kassite stela set up in a temple to record a grant of land.

■ c. 1154 BC
End of the Kassite empire. The cities around Babylon, which had been part of the Kassite empire, return to being ruled by local rulers. Many stone monuments, including the Code of Hammurabi, are carried off to the city of Susa in south-west Iran by the conquering Elamites.

A blue fluted glass bottle.

■ *c.* 1100 BC
The power of both the Assyrians and Babylonians declines as Mesopotamia is controlled by bands of invading Aramaeans (from the land west of Mesopotamia) and Chaldean nomads (who move into southern Mesopotamia).

■ *c.* 1000 BC
Iron was first smelted in Mesopotamia as early as 2000 BC but it only comes into widespread use after 1000 BC.

■ 934-912 BC
Reign of the Assyrian king Ashur-dan II. He rebuilds Assyrian cities, establishes strong control of his kingdom and increases the amount of farmland producing food.

■ 911-891 BC
Reign of the Assyrian king Adad-nirari II. He extends the territory controlled by Assyria.

This stone stela shows an Aramaean king. It was found near Damascus, a city in the Aramaeans' homeland west of Mesopotamia.

A bronze weight in the shape of lion from the Assyrian city of Kalhu (Nimrud).

ASSYRIAN EMPIRE 870 BC – 612 BC

A glazed tile showing king Ashurnasirpal II and his attendants.

■ *c.* 900 BC
The Chaldean people from southern Mesopotamia take control of Babylonia.

■ 883 – 859 BC
Reign of the Assyrian king Ashurnasirpal II. By the end of his reign, Assyria had recovered much of the territory that it had lost around 1100 BC.

A stela showing king Ashurnasirpal II.

A human-headed winged lion which stood at the entrance from a courtyard in the North-West Palace at Kalhu (Nimrud).

■ *c.* 721 – 705 BC
Reign of the Assyrian king Sargon II. During his reign a new capital city is founded at Dur-Sharrukin (also known as Khorsabad) to the north of the old capital at Nineveh. The city wall had seven gates leading into the city with its royal palace and temple complex.

■ 704 – 681 BC
Reign of the Assyrian king Sennacherib. During his reign the capital city of Assyria moves to Nineveh. The city is surrounded by a wall which runs for 12 km (7.5 miles) around the city. Sennacherib builds the South-west Palace, which is decorated with carved stone reliefs.

A fine pottery vessel from Nineveh.

NEO-BABYLONIAN EMPIRE 625 BC – 539

A carved stone relief showing the Assyrian king Ashurbanipal and queen Asur-sharratt.

■ **668 BC – 631 BC**
Reign of the Assyrian king Ashurbanipal. During his reign the Assyrian empire reaches its greatest extent.

■ **612 BC**
Nineveh, and other major Assyrian cities, are sacked by the Medes, from western Iran, and the Babylonians. They overthrow the Assyrian empire and divide it between themselves.

■ **587 BC**
Babylonian power extends and Nebuchadnezzar II captures Jerusalem.

■ **539 BC**
The Persian king Cyrus takes control of Babylon. Mesopotamia becomes part of the Achaemenid Persian empire.

■ **605 – 562 BC**
Reign of Chaldean king Nebuchadnezzar II. He rebuilds the city of Babylon, adding the Hanging Gardens of Babylon and monumental gates.

A modern half size reconstruction of the Ishtar Gate at Babylon.

A Babylonian map of the world, with Babylon at the centre.

■ 485 BC – 465 BC
Reign of the Persian king Xerxes.
Xerxes re-organizes his empire,
including Mesopotamia, into
provinces each ruled by a Persian
satrap (governor).

*Part of a stone relief from the Persian
kings' palace at Persepolis.*

*This stone relief comes from
one of the palaces at
Persepolis. It shows a guardian
figure in the form of a sphinx.*

■ 334 BC – 328 BC
The Persian empire, including
Mesopotamia, is conquered
by the Macedonian
king Alexander
who dies in
Babylon in 323 BC.

*Marble portrait
of Alexander.*

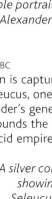

■ 312 BC
Babylon is captured
by Seleucus, one of
Alexander's generals,
who founds the
Seleucid empire.

*A silver coin
showing
Seleucus.*

■ *c.* 300 BC
Changes in the course of the River Euphrates and in the trade routes lead to the decline of the city of Ur, and the site is eventually abandoned as a place for people to live.

■ 141 BC
King Mithradates I from Parthia (Iran) conquers Mesopotamia and makes it part of the Parthian empire.

A silver coin showing Mithradates I.

■ AD 115-117
The Roman emperor Trajan conquers Mesopotamia, which becomes part of the Roman empire for a short time. Mesopotamia is returned to Parthian control by the emperor Hadrian in AD 117.

A gold coin showing the Roman emperor Trajan.

■ *c.* AD 150
Last known example of cuneiform writing is used in a Babylonian astronomy text.

■ AD 226-637
The Sasanian king Ardashir conquers the Parthian empire. Mesopotamia becomes part of the Sasanian empire which stretched from Mesopotamia into central Asia.

■ AD 637
Mesopotamia becomes part of the Islamic empire controlled by the Muslim Arabs.

A bronze figure of a Sasanian king.